A pastor, who is now in heaven, prayed publicly on the balcony of the opera house in Timisoara, reciting the 'Our Father'. The big desire then was that Bucharest would stand with us against Communism and that happened on 21st December. From that day we knew that Communism had begun to fall.

Then and Now

I was not a Christian then, having grown up in a non-Christian family. I didn't know anything about Jesus, although I knew there was a God because I had a grandfather who taught me the 'Our Father' prayer. He was my father's father and he led the singing in an Orthodox church. From about ten years old and onwards I remember struggling to understand what the goal of my life was. My father was a mayor and a member of the Communist Party. His goal in life was to rise socially and do something good.

In Communist times people were normally very poor but, because my father was a Communist and a mayor, we could have things other people could not. I remember being in very long queues to get chocolate. We would rise at 4 am to go for milk and there would already be a big queue when we got there.

No one would jump the queue because we were all afraid of being reported. I grew up with fear. At home we were told that we had to be careful because microphones could be anywhere. People lived in a state of constant fear.

When I was twelve years old my father used his influence to move me from our village to a city school. It was very hard because I was put in a family I didn't know. I had to eat when I was told, to do what I was told. That left me with another fear, the fear of hunger. I still sometimes have it when the fridge is empty.

'Our Father'

Always before going to bed I prayed the 'Our Father' prayer as my father's father taught me. And, if I didn't pray, I wouldn't sleep. I went on vacation with my grandfather in the summers and he always took me to church on Sundays. I sat beside him while he sang.

Our Father in heaven,

Hallowed be Your name.

Your kingdom come.

Your will be done

On earth as it is in heaven.

Give us day by day our daily bread.

And forgive us our sins,

For we also forgive everyone who is indebted to us.

And do not lead us into temptation,

But deliver us from the evil one.

(Luke 11: 2-4)

    I said the 'Our Father' prayer but did not know the meaning of it and didn't think of the words. Also, when I had an exam I went into the Orthodox Church where there was a saint, Saint Anton, who was a miracle maker. I thought that, if I took his books and touched his coffin, I would be helped. Although I wasn't an atheist I didn't know that God has a Son who can give us salvation.

A Clever Rebel

I loved physics and was in third position in the whole of Romania in 6th and 7th grade in physics competitions. It was my desire to study physics. My father tried to encourage me to do medicine, but I had developed a little rebellion towards him because he would push me to do things without explaining them to me. I made mistakes with that rebellion because some of his advice was good. One of the things I rebelled against was his idea of studying medicine.

My father was smarter than me. He made an arrangement to take me to Tirgu-Mures to meet a medical student and to see the university. They took me to classes and I remember us going into the morgue where the students were dissecting, and I loved it! That was a turning point and I decided I would do medicine, which is why I was in Timisoara at the time of the revolution in 1989.

Besides being a student I worked as a nurse to support myself. After that I did a one year internship and then specialised in pulmonology – how to treat lung disease – for two years. I graduated in 1992 and then worked as a resident doctor and also taught in the nursing school to earn enough to live.

In 1995 I went to the United States to a conference. While I was there I decided to contact someone I knew and we visited places together. When my money ran out I asked her to help me find a job. At that time she still hadn't passed her exams to become a doctor in the United States and she was working with old people, cleaning and doing things like that.

The Promised Land!

Coming from my background I felt that the US was the promised land! I thought I could work there for a few months and make money. Eventually, I found a weekend job working in a nursing home owned by a Romanian couple. When I was given $100 for working two days, I said, 'Wow, that's my salary for two months at home!'

    A few days later they offered me a full-time job, staying in the home, and caring for the six residents. These elderly ladies loved me and began to teach me English. The owners were Christians and they went to a Baptist church. I remember seeing them on Sundays going to church together with their child nicely dressed and I just loved that. My need of love and seeing a happy family touched me. I asked them how they kept their relationship right. You see, while I was a student my heart had been broken and so I didn't believe that there were men who could be honest and loving. When I saw that couple I really loved what I saw. Even today that motivates me in how I am in my relationship with my husband.

Who is Jesus?

One day I asked them how they could love each other and be so nice with each other. The husband told me, 'It's not us. We are just normal people. It's Jesus.' And I said, 'Who is Jesus?' So that was the beginning. He began telling me who Jesus is although it didn't make much sense to me. He also introduced me to the concept of sin and told me that sinners go to hell. I didn't see myself as a sinner because I was brought up to be a good person, helping others, helping colleagues, respecting my parents, respecting work and so on. We had these values.

I began reading the gospels but didn't understand anything. After reading the Bible I remember saying that I didn't know what it was about. My friends told me to pray and read the Bible three times a day and I did exactly what I was told. As I saw how they prayed, I tried to do the same. To me their praying seemed very aggressive. After I was invited to their prayer group where they prayed loudly standing up, I confronted them. I said, 'You're praying just for me to see you.' I was critical, but open and very honest with everything. They were patient with me and told me that I needed to keep reading the Bible. That was 1995.

For Your goodness' sake, O LORD.
Good and upright is the LORD;
Therefore He teaches sinners in the way.
The humble He guides in justice,
And the humble He teaches His way.
All the paths of the LORD are mercy and truth,
To such as keep His covenant and His testimonies.
For Your name's sake, O LORD,
Pardon my iniquity, for it is great.
(Psalm 25:4-11)

A New Person

When Jesus forgives our sins, our lives are changed. Back in Timisoara in the winter of 1998, I began to help children who were living on the street – children whom I would never have spoken to before I became a Christian. I am a doctor and my husband is a teacher. Together we continue to take the opportunities that God gives us to tell children that Jesus is the one and only Saviour, the one and only way to heaven.

In the Bible, the apostle Paul says: 'I can do everything through Christ who gives me strength.' As a Christian I have learned not to depend on what I can do but to put myself into the hand of God. Now that I am a child of God, I am a new person and, if he calls me to do something, even though I don't have the resources, it can be done. It's not me – it's Christ that lives in me.
Jesus can change you, too. He can forgive your sins and make you right with God. Pray to him now! Dare to ask the Lord to help you with whatever problems you have. He will answer you. He has promised that he will not turn away anyone who comes to him.

Back in Romania

I was there for six months and then came back to Romania and used my money to buy an apartment. When I was in the US I applied for a scholarship. After eight months in Romania I received an answer and was accepted. Then I went back to the States, but this time I went to Rochester, New York. I questioned why there are so many religions when there is only one God. I had a fear of hell and became determined to find out the truth but still I had no awareness of the goodness of Jesus.

A Wrong Turning

During my eight months in Romania I went to the Orthodox church, a Pentecostal church, a Seventh Day Adventist church and to the Jehovah Witnesses too.

I was in all of them at the same time. When I went back to the US I became very active in the Jehovah Witnesses and asked for baptism. They wanted to know if I celebrated Christmas, and I said that I did. Then they asked if I celebrated my birthday, and I told them I did. The third thing they wanted to know was whether I would do blood transfusions. I replied that I would because I was a doctor and I believed I could do transfusions. The elders told me that wasn't allowed. After that interview they refused me, telling me I needed to study the Watchtower more until I clarified these subjects. I was broken-hearted that day.

to West Side Baptist Church in Rochester (now Journey Church) and I went with her. When I felt the peace there I just burst into tears and said, 'This is my place.' It was so overwhelming. Right away I understood that God is the Father and, if I believed in Jesus his Son, I'd be saved. All that knowledge came to my heart, a totally broken heart. I understood Jesus saved me. He forgave my sins and made me his child. Immediately I joined every prayer group and every Bible study possible. I spent most of my time working in a hospital. Life was church, hospital, church. That was all; there was nothing else.

I found a wonderful fellowship group and a prayer and Bible study group, but I couldn't find an opportunity to serve. Later on in my prayer group I heard that the church had a place that ministered to downtown children and they needed help. It was called Rochester Family Mission. I went there but, when I saw the people were black, I didn't want to help. In my heart I felt a resentment toward gypsies that came from my childhood in Romania. That was a Communist way of thinking. I went to the pastor a little fearfully and said I didn't want to go, but was told to apply. At the end of my interview they assured me I was exactly the person they needed.

A Change of Attitude

Eventually, the hospital agreed that I could work extra hours on other days so that on Wednesdays I was free for Rochester Family Mission. And so after a few months in the church I began helping in their Wednesday programme although I had no previous experience of working with children.

As I spent more time in the Word of God and going to church, I began seeing inside myself, seeing what I hadn't seen before. I called myself a good person but, when I started really studying the Bible, I realised what I really was like. When we call ourselves good we are using human standards and not comparing ourselves against the Bible's standards. But when we start reading the Bible and learn God's standards, we see how bad we are. I saw that I didn't love these people, that I was judging them and criticising them. These are things that God doesn't love and he opened my eyes to see that.

I began to love these children. Working with them helped me to grow up as a Christian. While we developed the club I did gymnastics with them and ate breakfast and lunch with them, sometimes feeding them. I helped with their maths and told them a Bible story. As I did every single little thing with them, I began to love them more. The wall between me and them broke and it was God who broke it down.

A Prayer for Forgiveness

Show me Your ways, O LORD;

Teach me Your paths.

Lead me in Your truth and teach me,

For You are the God of my salvation;

On You I wait all the day.

Remember, O LORD, Your tender mercies and Your lovingkindnesses,

For they are from of old.

Do not remember the sins of my youth, nor my transgressions;

According to Your mercy remember me,